MW00897994

THE BORROWERS

by
Mary Norton

Teacher Guide

Written by:
Anne Troy

Note

The Voyager/HBJ paperback edition of the book published by Harcourt Brace Jovanovich was used to prepare this teacher guide. The page references may differ in the hardcover or other paperback editions.

ISBN 1-56137-069-X

To order, contact your local school supply store, or—

Novel Units, Inc.
P.O. Box 791610
San Antonio, TX 78279

Table of Contents

Skills and Strategies

Thinking
  Comparing and contrasting,
  evaluating, analyzing details,
  synthesizing ideas

Comprehension
  Predicting, sequencing,
  cause/effect

Writing
  Narrative

Vocabulary
  Antonym/synonym, context

Listening/Speaking
  Participation in discussion,
  drama

Literary Elements
  Character, plot, setting,
  conflict

Summary

People often put things away carefully and remember exactly where they put them. Why do they mysteriously disappear, and where have they gone? In *The Borrowers,*Mary Norton gives the answer to this puzzle. The Borrowers were creatures who lived in a world of their own under the floorboards, along the pipes, under the clocks, and on the mantels of homes. Children will identify with the problems of Arrietty, the only child of the little people under the floorboards.

Instructions Prior to Reading

Setting the Purpose:

Instruct the children that this is a fantasy. Ask them to give other words that mean fantasy, and give other examples of fantasy.

Recommended Procedure:

The book will be read one chapter at a time, using DRTA (Directed Reading Thinking Activity) Method. This technique involves reading a section, predicting what will happen next (making good guesses) based on what has already occurred in the story. The children continue to read and everyone verifies his/her predictions.

Story Map:

See page 6 of this guide.

This activity is designed to help children recognize various kinds of story structures, to make inferences, to recognize character traits and relationships among the characters.

1. Who is the main character? (Write the name in the center of a large sheet of paper.)

2. What is he/she like? Look for information in conversation, speech, thoughts, and deeds.

3. Who else do you think might be important in the story? (Write the names spaced around the main character's name.)

Using Predictions in the Novel Unit Approach

We all make predictions as we read—little guesses about what will happen next, how the conflict will be resolved, which details given by the author will be important to the plot, which details will help to fill in our sense of a character. Students should be encouraged to predict, to make sensible guesses. As students work on predictions, these discussion questions can be used to guide them: What are some of the ways to predict? What is the process of a sophisticated reader's thinking and predicting? What clues does an author give us to help us in making our predictions? Why are some predictions more likely than others?

A predicting chart is for students to record their predictions. As each subsequent chapter is discussed, you can review and correct previous predictions. This procedure serves to focus on predictions and to review the stories.

Use the facts and ideas the author gives.

Use your own knowledge.

Use new information that may cause you to change your mind.

Predictions:

_____

_____

_____

_____

Prediction Chart

What characters have we met so far?	What is the conflict in the story?	What are your predictions?	Why did you make those predictions?

Story Map

Characters_____

_____

_____

Setting →

Time and Place_____

_____

_____

Problem →

Problem_____

_____

_____

_____

Goal →

Goal_____

_____

_____

_____

Episodes →

Beginning ——→ Development ——→ Outcome

_____

_____

_____

_____

_____

_____

_____

_____

Resolution →

Resolution_____

_____

_____

_____

_____

_____

Problems

There are flashbacks and a story within a story in *The Borrowers*. These are hard for students to understand without a time chart.

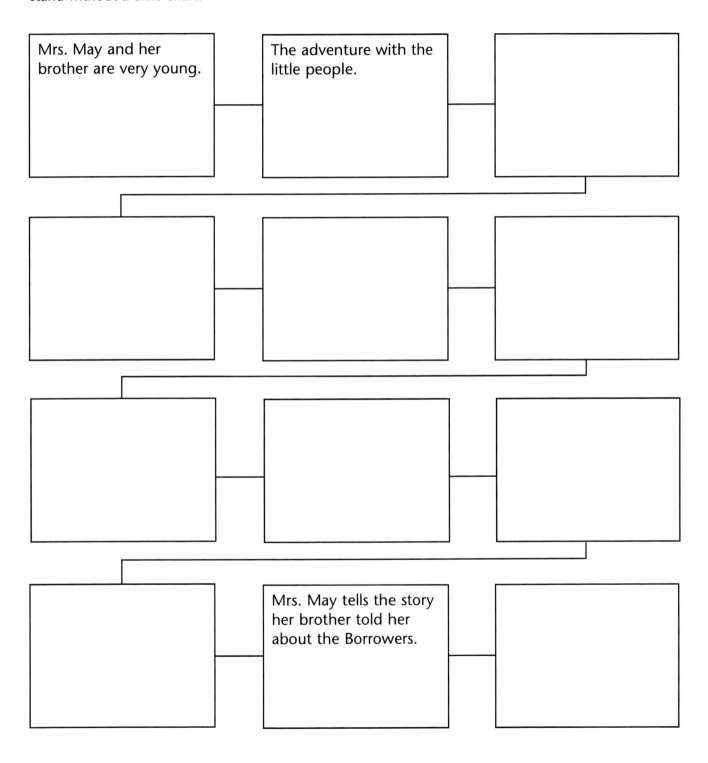

Box 1: Mrs. May and her brother are very young.

Box 2: The adventure with the little people.

Box (bottom middle): Mrs. May tells the story her brother told her about the Borrowers.

Chapter 1: pp. 3-12

Vocabulary:

marmalade (3)	crochet (3)	conceited (8)
intervals (9)	wainscot (12)	

Discussion Questions:

1. Where did the Borrowers get their names? (*p. 8 They borrowed them.*)

2. What kind of personalities did they have? (*p. 8 Touchy and conceited, and they thought they owned the world; frightened.*)

3. Who are the main characters? Begin an Attribute Web for Arrietty. See bottom of this page and page 9.

4. Where does the story take place? Did the clues in the front cover and end papers help you make an accurate prediction about the setting?

5. At the end of each chapter list the major event in the chapter on the story map (page 6).

6. Develop a Cause and Effect Map for each chapter (see page 10).

7. What do you think the big problem of this novel will be? (**Prediction:** *Answers will vary.*)

Special Activities:

Do you ever lose things in your house? Make a list of objects missed by the class. What do you think happens to them? Keep a list of items that the little people borrow in this book. How did they use each item in their house?

Using Character Attribute Webs in the Novel Units Approach:

Attribute webs are simply a visual representation of a character from the novel. They provide a systematic way for the students to organize and recap the information they have about a particular character. Attribute webs may be used after reading the novel to recapitulate information about a particular character or completed gradually as information unfolds, done individually, or finished as a group project.

One type of character attribute web uses these divisions:

- How a character looks. (Close your eyes and picture the character. Describe him.)

- Where a character lives. (Where and when does the character live?)

- How a character acts and feels. (How does the character feel in this picture? How would you feel if this happened to you? How do you think the character feels?)

- How others feel about the character. (How does another specific character feel about our character?)

In this group discussion about the student attribute webs and specific characters, the teacher can ask for backup proof from the novel.

Attribute Webs need not be confined to characters. They may also be used to organize information about a concept, object or place.

Acts	Feels

1. _____
2. _____
3. _____
4. _____

1. _____
2. _____
3. _____
4. _____

Character

Looks	Says

1. _____
2. _____
3. _____
4. _____

1. _____
2. _____
3. _____
4. _____

Cause/Effect Map:

To plot cause and effect in a story, first list the sequence of events. Then mark causes with a "C" and effects with an "E." Use an arrow from the cause to the effect. Remember that many effects cause something else so they might be marked with an "E" and a "C" with an arrow to the next effect.

Events in the story

1.

2.

3.

4.

5.

6.

7.

8.

9.

10.

Another way to map cause and effect is to look for an effect and then backtrack to the single or multiple causes.

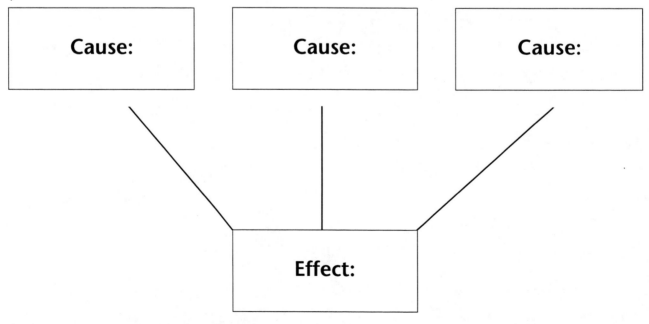

Chapter 2: pp. 13-22

Vocabulary:

      lacquer (15)   statuary (18)

Discussion Questions:

  1.   Make a list of unusual names in this book.

  2.   Why do you think the Borrowers were frightened?
      Prediction: What might happen to them?

  3.   Do any characters act in ways which are unexpected or surprising? (*Adults are frightened.*)

Art Activity:

Pick out the unusual furnishings in the illustrations on pages 16-17. There are many descriptions that are not illustrated. Draw an unusual scene that will give the "flavor" of the book, e.g. Arrietty rolling the potato.

Chapter 3: pp. 23-26

Vocabulary:

      foraged(23)   bit-bucket (23)   vibration (26)

  1.   Were there any incidents that were funny?

  2.   Why was Homily so worried? (*Something might have happened to Pod.*)

  3.   Eggletina and Uncle Hendreary are mentioned. Where do you suppose they are? What is their story? (**Prediction:** *Answers will vary.*)

Chapter 4: pp. 27-34

Vocabulary:

      mechanically (28)   groping (28)   emigrate (29)
      badger (29)   draughts (30)

Discussion Questions:

  1.   What was the size of the doll's tea cup? (*Teacher may display a tiny cup.*)

  2.   What did Pod mean by "I been seen"? (*People saw Pod.*) Why was that so awful?

  3.   Where do Hendreary and Lupy live? (*p. 29 In a badger's set among earthworms.*)

  4.   What is so bad about Hendreary and Lupy's life? (*p. 30 They eat nuts, berries, and even mice. They have draughts and fresh air.*)

5. What did the boy do? *(p. 32 He took the cup away from Pod until he got down the curtain.)*

6. Again the Borrowers mention Hendreary and they got a cat. Is that a clue? What do you think happened now?

7. What do you think Pod and Homily mean when they say "Well, they hadn't told her...That's where they went wrong"?

8. What do you think Homily and Pod will tell Arrietty?

Art Activity:
On page 29, the illustrator has a picture of Papa. What do you think he looks like? Draw a picture and begin an attribute web on all of Pod's characteristics (see pages 8 and 9).

Chapter 5: pp. 35-44

Vocabulary:

crouched (35)	faltered (38)	crumpets (43)
sillabub (43)	parquet (44)	

Discussion Questions:
1. Why did Arrietty's parents get her out of bed? *(p. 44 To tell her about Eggletina and some of the other little people who lived in the house, and to tell her about UPSTAIRS.)*

2. Why did the other little people leave? *(pp. 42-43 Some of the rooms were not used so they had no food and it was cold.)*

Chapter 6: pp. 45-54

Vocabulary:

ventured (48)	cooped up (49)	ecstatic (51)
hankering (52)	conviction (52)	

Discussion Questions:
1. What were the gates in the passages for? *(p. 46 To keep out mice and rats and to keep Arrietty in.)*

2. What happened to Eggletina? *(p. 47 Cat probably got her.)*

3. Why did they tell Arrietty about Eggletina? *(p. 48 Because Pod had been "seen.")*

4. Why didn't Arrietty like staying in the house? *(No one to talk to; they lived under the floor; no one to play with; nothing to see but dust and passage; no light except candlelight, fire and light through cracks.)*

Chapter 7: pp. 55-63

Vocabulary:

essentials (55)   singed (56)   inferno (56)   retorted (57)

Discussion Questions:

1. Why did Pod and Homily decide to let Arrietty start learning to borrow? *(p. 52 In case any thing happened to them.)*

2. Why did Pod stick to kitchen borrowing? *(p. 55 For bare essentials of fuel and food, because he had been "seen.")*

3. What did Arrietty see for the first time? *(pp. 60-62 Sun, clock, rugs, the open front door and beyond, grass and sky.)*

Chapter 8: pp. 64-70

Vocabulary:

embedded (66)   antennae (68)   gnarled (69)

Discussion Questions:

1. What big adventures does Arrietty have?

2. The last sentence in the chapter has suspense. "Something had glittered. Arrietty stared." What do you think will happen? (**Prediction:** *Answers will vary.*)

Writing Activity:

Suppose you had a magic ring that would make you two inches tall for one hour if you rubbed it once, or ten feet tall for one hour if you rubbed it twice. (When the hour is up, you would be the size you are now—until you rubbed the ring again.) Write a story telling what happened to you while you were two inches tall. What were some of the advantages? What were the dangers? What did you do? Or, if you prefer, write about your adventures while you were ten feet tall.

Chapter 9: pp. 71-79

Vocabulary:

faltered (75)   appease (76)   exaggerated (79)

Discussion Questions:

1. Who saw Arrietty? Check your predictions.

Drama Activity:

The boy and Arrietty had a conversation. In small groups, role play the conversation. If you were Arrietty what would you talk about with the giant boy?

Chapter 10: pp. 80-89

Vocabulary:

exploits (80)   decanter (81)

Discussion Questions:

1. Why does Great Aunt Sophy think that Pod comes out of the Madeira bottle?

2. Why do you think the boy talks to Arrietty?

3. What did Arrietty learn? (*There are millions of humans and they are not dying off.*)

4. Why did Arrietty cry? (*p. 86 The boy said the Borrowers were dying off and Arrietty would be the last one.*)

5. What does Arrietty say is the difference between borrowing and stealing? What do you say?

Chapter 11: pp. 90-95

Vocabulary:

sarcastic (93)

Discussion Questions:

1. Why do you suppose Arrietty did not tell her parents about the boy?

2. Why did Arrietty write the letter? (*To find out if her relatives were alive.*) What do you think will happen? (**Prediction:** *Answers will vary.*)

Chapter 12: pp. 96-104

Vocabulary:

pilaster (98)   lissom (98)   trice (99)
javelin (99)   ferret (101)   scullery (104)

Discussion Questions:

1. Arrietty had problems getting out of her safe world. What did Homily really want that made Pod go UPSTAIRS? (*p. 98 Blotting paper.*)

2. Why couldn't Arrietty give the letter to the boy? (*Her parents watched all the time.*)

3. What did Arrietty learn from listening to Mrs. Driver and Crampfurl? (*The boy is looking for her little relatives. He keeps lifting the mat looking for her note.*)

4. What do you think Arrietty must do? What will happen?

Chapter 13: pp. 105-113

Vocabulary:

barrier (108)　　　　shrouded (109)　　　　obscured (109)　　　　plateau (109)

Discussion Questions:

1. What was Arrietty worried about? *(p. 106 Seeing the boy; being the last Borrower.)*

2. What message did the boy have? *(p. 111 Tell your Aunt Lupy to come home.)* What do you think that meant?

Chapter 14: pp. 114-119

Vocabulary:

imperative (116)　　　soberly (119)

Discussion Questions:

1. How did Pod and Homily act after they discovered that Arrietty was talking to the boy? *(Very frightened.)*

2. Why is Pod so upset? *(p. 117 No human being has ever known where the Borrowers lived.)*

3. What are human beans? *(p. 119 Human beings.)*

4. What will the boy do next? *(**Prediction:** Answers will vary.)*

Chapter 15: pp. 120-129

Vocabulary:

golliwog (121)　　　　turmoil (123)　　　　gingerly (125)　　　　ecstatically (125)
placatingly (126)　　　presumably (126)　　vigorously (129)

Discussion Questions:

1. What was the most exciting part of this chapter? *(The boy broke into the Borrowers house with a screwdriver.)*

2. Why did the boy do this? *(pp. 125-129, To bring them furniture.)*

Chapter 16: pp. 130-137

Vocabulary:

phase (130)	disheveled (131)	endeavor (135)	whorls (135)
eddies (135)	staid (135)	irked (135)	depleted (136)
calculated (136)	cackle (137)		

Discussion Questions:

1. How did life change for the Borrowers? *(The boy brought treasures.)*

2. How did the Borrowers repay the boy? *(p. 131, Arrietty read to him.)*

3. What did Arrietty learn? *(Everything did not revolve around the little people.)*

4. What was the Borrowers' one sadness? *(p. 133, No other little people were there to admire their treasures.)*

5. How did Pod feel about all this? *(p. 132, He got tired rearranging the furniture.)*

6. **Prediction:** What was going to get the Borrowers in trouble? *(p. 134, The boy taking things from the glass cabinet.)*

7. Who is going to catch them? *(**Prediction:** Answers will vary.)*

Chapter 17: pp. 138-145

Discussion Questions:

1. How did Mrs. Driver try to catch the thieves?

2. Was this chapter exciting? Was there suspense? How did the author do this?

Chapter 18: pp. 146-156

Vocabulary:

assent (149)	tremulous (151)	appeased (152)	malicious (154)
noxious (154)	dribbet (154)	crafty (155)	

Discussion Questions:

1. Is there a villain in this story? Brainstorm the word villain. Who could the villain be? The boy, Crampfurl, or Mrs. Driver? Or are the Borrowers villains? How could this be?

Chapter 19: pp. 157-171

Vocabulary:

    rendered (159)   neutral (159)   rapt (165)

Discussion Questions:

1. This is a story within a story. Mrs. May is telling Kate a story that her brother told her. Do you know any other stories like this?

2. What did the policeman think about the little people story? *(p. 159, Mrs. Driver had chased him and called him a thief when he was a little boy. He thought that Mrs. Driver had had too much wine.)*

3. Was the cat a help for Mrs. Driver? *(p. 160, The cat only had two ideas— to get out of the house or to get into the larder.)*

4. What did Aunt Sophy mean when she said, "If you don't like them...keep the bottle corked"? *(p. 162, She thought that Mrs. Driver had been drinking too much so she's telling her to stop.)*

5. Why do you think the boy took the pick-ax and smashed the grating? *(p. 171, To give the Borrowers a way out.)*

Chapter 20: pp. 172-180

Vocabulary:

    stoats (174)   haws (175)

Discussion Questions:

1. Mrs. May had her ideas of what happened to the Borrowers. What did she do for them? *(p.177, Took all the furniture from the doll house plus things she bought for them to a place where she thought they might be and left the treasures. The next day they were gone.)*

Post-reading Activities

1. There are no chapter titles. Make titles that will list the main events.

2. How did the characters change during the story? How would you explain the changes? *(Arrietty learned about the world and human beings. All the Borrowers had contact with the boy and Mrs. Driver until they had to leave the house.)*

3. Who do you think the main character was? What did he/she learn?

4. Was there a villain in the story? What role does this villain play in the sequence of events? How would the story be different if Mrs. Driver was not in the story?

5. How was the setting important?

6. What do you think is the most important thing to remember in the story?

Activity Sheet: What's In The Room?

Choose a room found generally in every house or apartment, and have the children list items which they know might be found in that room: kitchen, dining room, living room. Or a child can have the other children guess what room he is thinking of by naming the items it might contain. This may not be as easy as it seems, since rugs, tables, and dishes are found in many rooms.

Art Activity:

We have an empty doll house. Suppose this was a new house for the Borrowers. What kind of furniture could you make for them? Could you help fix our doll house for them? Make a list of items that the little people "borrowed." How did they use each item in their home? Make some original furniture for them out of unusual materials.

Writing Activity:

A) Make up a new adventure for *The Borrowers*.

B) Write a different ending for *The Borrowers*.

Drama Activity:

Act out the following scenes:

A) Arrietty meeting the boy.

B) Pod talking to Aunt Sophy.

C) Mrs. Driver and Crampfurl in the kitchen.

Point of View:

Divide the class into small groups. Each person in each group should tell the story from a different point of view, e.g. the boy's, Mrs. Driver's, Aunt Sophy's. Encourage the children to imitate the characters they choose with voice and gestures.

Hangman:

Using the vocabulary words which have been introduced, think of a word and draw blanks to represent the number of letters in that word. Draw a noose on the board. (This may be a simple number 7 with a rope dangling from it.) The child must guess which letters are in the word.

When a child guesses a correct letter, fill it in its proper place. If a child guesses a wrong letter, draw one part of a stick figure man under the noose until a whole body is completed. The parts which may be drawn on the figure are a head, a line for the body, arms, legs, hands, feet, eyes, a nose and a mouth. If there are double letters in the word, both should be filled in.

If the body is completed before the word is guessed, the teacher (or leader) wins. If the word is guessed before the body is completed, the children are the winners. The child who guesses the word may take the teacher's place.

Word Pantomime:

Whisper a descriptive word to a child to pantomime. You might tell the child to act tired, angry or hungry. The student acts the word out for the rest of the class. When someone guesses the word, he has a chance to think of a word and to pantomime it. The Vocabulary Words for each story are a good source for pantomimes.

Alliterative Add-A-Word:

This game helps the children to appreciate the many ways in which the same initial letter can combine with others to form different sounds and words. The first player begins a sentence. Each player will add one word. Thus, if adjectives are being added in a sentence, the description might look something like this:

Jane is _____ artful, able, alert, attentive, active, amiable.

Each player is given only a limited amount of time to think of another word to add to his list. When no one can do so, a new list is begun with the next letter in the alphabet.

Listening Activities:

- What classroom noises are distracting to you? Make a list. Tell which is the most distracting noise and explain why in a short paragraph. How can you overcome these distractions?

- Prepare a description of your favorite character or scene in the book. Read those descriptions to classmates who will try to identify them.

- Listen for details as the teacher or a classmate reads a favorite part of the story. After you've listened to the whole passage, describe the details.

- Listen to this novel and in other readings for "sound words." Then make up stories using the sound words. Examples might be sounds you like: morning sounds, evening sounds, sounds at the supper table, winter sounds, television sounds, or sounds on a playground.

- Read poems with word patterns in them and ask the students to listen for them. Look in the novel for word patterns. Discuss why authors use word patterns in stories.

- Listen to a recording or read aloud a portion of the book with vivid descriptions. Ask the students to picture in their minds what they are hearing.

- Have a panel discussion with classmates as panelists on how to be a good listener.

Special Activities

Logical Placement:

Take major happenings from the story map and write on strips of paper to form an out-of-order story. The children must put the events in chronological order.

Opposites:
Using words from the novel, the first child on one team says an adjective or an adverb. He might say "best." The first member of the opposing team must quickly give the antonym. In this case the word would be "worst."

Name of the Game:
This game is particularly helpful in the beginning of the year to familiarize the children with each other's names. With younger children, split the class into four or five groups. Each group should form a circle, then line up alphabetically, according to their first or last names. The first group that is ready and correct wins.

With older children, split the class into two teams and have each team line up alphabetically on opposite sides of the room. Or pass a complete list of the class to each student and have him number the names in alphabetical order.

Similar Words:
Say or write a word on the board, and have the children write as many synonyms for it as they can. If there is extra time, have the children either find opposites for each word or put them in alphabetical order. Let the children use their dictionaries on some occasions.

Vocabulary Activities:
1. Develop word maps. Use color to distinguish antonyms, synonyms, etc.

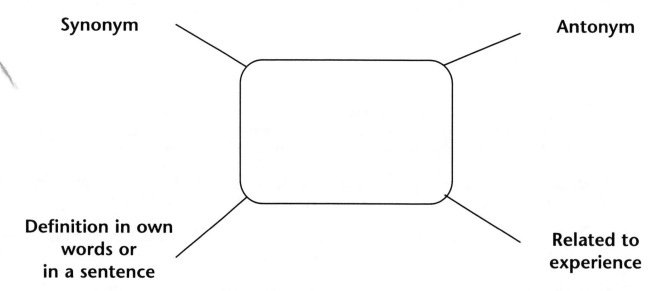

Synonym

Antonym

Definition in own words or in a sentence

Related to experience

2. Crossword Puzzles—Have students use vocabulary words from the chapter to make crossword puzzles on graph paper. They should write a question for each word and develop an answer sheet. The teacher will check and then distribute the puzzles to other students to work out in their free time.

3. One student picks a word from the vocabulary list or cards. Another student has ten (or five) questions to discover the word and give the definition.

4.   List vocabulary words on large sheets of paper. Leave space for students to a) illustrate the meaning next to each word; b) list a memory device to remember the word.

5.   List the vocabulary words on the board or on a sheet of paper in the form of a table. Pronounce the words. Ask the students to rate their knowledge of each of the words (as a group, in cooperative groups or individually.)

Vocabulary Word	I can define	I have heard/seen	I don't know

6.   Provide vocabulary challenge words in context. Ask students to "guess" at the meaning from context, asking why for each guess. Generate a listing of the "why" answers to teach context clues.

7.   Select ten words. Write only every other letter and a synonym or definition. Exchange student papers. Example: a_o_a: (aroma).

8.   Word Sort:
          I can say
          I know what it means
          I do not know

9.   Word Sort:
          Action
          Things
          Places
          Names

10.   I am thinking of a word that:
          has a long a sound
          begins with the same sound as Pat
          means _____
          is a synonym of

Activity Sheet

Vocabulary

marmalade	crochet	intervals
conceited	wainscot	lacquer
statuary	foraged	bit-bucket
mechanically	groping	emigrated
badger	draughts	crouched
faltered	crumpets	sillabub
parquet	ventured	cooped up

Activity Sheet

Vocabulary

estatic	hankering	conviction
essentials	singed	inferno
retorted	embedded	antennae
gnarled	faltered	appease
exaggerated	exploits	decanter
sarcastic	pilaster	lissom
trice	javelin	ferret

Activity Sheet

Vocabulary

scullery	barrier	shrouded
obscured	plateau	imperative
soberly	golliwog	turmoil
gingerly	estatically	placatingly
presumably	vigorously	phase
disheveled	endeavor	whorls
eddies	staid	irked

Activity Sheet

Vocabulary

depleted	calculated	cackle
assent	tremulous	appeased
malicious	noxious	dribbet
crafty	rendered	neutral
rapt	stoats	haws

Assessment for *The Borrowers*

Assessment is an on-going process, more than a quiz at the end of the book. Points may be added to show the level of achievement. When an item is completed, the teacher and the student check it.

Name _____ Date _____

Student   **Teacher**

_____   _____   1.   Complete the story map.

_____   _____   2.   Make attribute webs for the main characters.

_____   _____   3.   The boy and Arrietty had a conversation. With a classmate role play this conversation.

_____   _____   4.   Make a collage about this novel. Include important symbols and words that summarize the story.

_____   _____   5.   Create a shoe box diorama of your favorite scene fromthe story. Label with a short description.

_____   _____   6.   Write chapter titles that either indicate something that might happen or create suspense to encourage the reader.

_____   _____   7.   Make a four-panel cartoon strip of an important incident in the novel and quote conversation from the novel in balloons above the speakers.

_____   _____   8.   Sketch a family portrait of the Borrowers.

_____   _____   9.   What is a heroine? Is there a heroine in this novel? Why or why not? Write a short paper of explanation.

_____   _____   10.   Change three things in this novel and explain to a classmate how the changes would make a difference.

Notes

Notes

28